9000979507

The Look Book

Chris Sickels
AKA
Red Nose Studio

HOW books
Cincinnati, Ohio
www.howdesign.com

The illustrations in this book are three-dimensional sets shot on Fujichrome Provia 100F with a Horseman 4x5 camera. The text was handwritten with Hunt 108 pen nibs and Higgins waterproof black ink on paper. The typeface used is Cochin LT Std.

Published by HOW Books, an imprint of F+W Publications, Inc., 4700 East Galbraith Road, Cincinnati, Ohio 45236. (800) 289-0963. First edition.

11 10 09 08 07 5 4 3 2 1

Distributed in Canada by Fraser Direct, 100 Armstrong Avenue, Georgetown, Ontario, Canada L7G 5S4, Tel: (905) 877-4411.

Distributed in the U.K. and Europe by David & Charles, Brunel House, Newton Abbot, Devon, TQ12 4PU, England, Tel: (+44) 1626-323200, Fax: (+44) 1626-323319, E-mail: postmaster@davidandcharles.co.uk.

Distributed in Australia by Capricorn Link, P.O. Box 704, Windsor, NSW 2756 Australia, Tel: (02) 4577-3555.

Library of Congress Cataloging-in-Publication Data

Sickels, Chris.
The look book / by Chris Sickels, [dba] Red Nose Studio.
p. cm.
ISBN-13: 978-1-58180-940-4 (alk. paper)
ISBN-10: 1-58180-940-9
1. English language--Homonyms--Juvenile literature. I. Red Nose Studio. II. Title.
PE1595.S53 2007
428.1--dc22 2007008571

Edited by Amy Schell
Designed by Grace Ring
Production coordinated by Greg Nock

To Jennifer + Owen
for helping me sea differently.

To Mrs. Martin who knew my
drawings could take me places

Only a week into summer vacation, Ian and Ann had played all the games in the game closet, read all the books on the bookshelf, and watched all the TV they could stand.

One morning, Ian looked at Ann
and Ann looked at Ian.
They shrugged their shoulders
and sighed.

"I'm bored," said Ian.
"I'm bored," said Ann.

"We're bored," they complained to their mother.

"Bored?!" she cried.

"Why, just go outside and look around.
There's plenty to see!"

Ann looked at Ian and
Ian looked at Ann.
They shrugged their shoulders
and headed out the door.

Ann saw a

whole pie

Ian saw a
pie hole

FINE
MEATS!

Ian saw a man that needed to mince something.

Ann saw a man
that needed mints
or something

SHRO

Ian saw a dog
throw up a baseball

Ann saw a dog
throw a baseball up

Ian saw a car
get towed

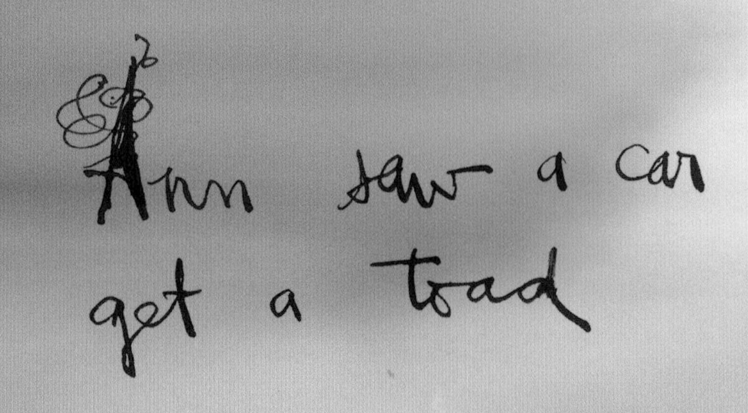
Ann saw a car
get a toad

Ann saw a squirrel
shaped like a gourd

Ian saw a squirrel
get gored by a shape

Stan saw a man
who'd lost his sole

Ann saw a man
who'd lost his soul

Ian saw a bird
soar overhead

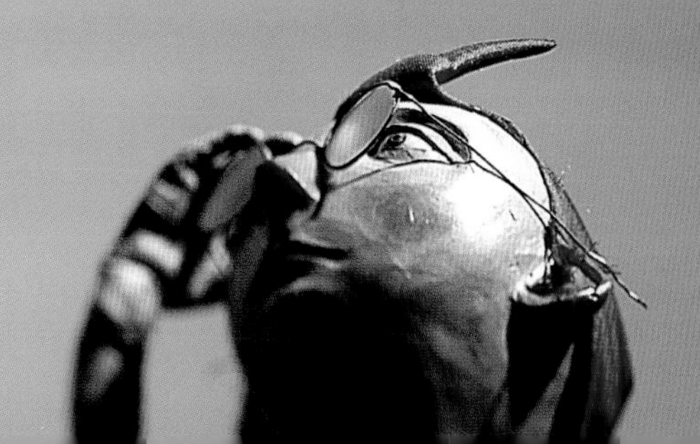

Ann saw a bird
with a sore head

Ann saw a man
with a pet beet

Ian saw a man
beat his pet

So Amn saw a woman who
had been to the mall

GODDESS

Ian saw a man who
had been mauled

Ann saw a man
allude great things

Ian saw a man
elude great things

Ian saw a priest
exorcising

Ann saw a priest
exercising

Ann saw someone
at peace

Ian saw a piece
of someone

Ann saw a man wail

MY

Ian saw a whale man

Ian saw someone
had left his bear behind

FREE BIRD

Ann saw someone
had left his behind bare

Ann saw someone
had cut her hair

Pan saw someone
had cut her hare

Ian saw a kitchen sink

Ann saw a kitchen sink

"When they'd seen all they could see
and the sun was getting low,
Ian and Ann headed for home.

As they walked through the door
their mother smiled
and asked brightly:

'So, what did you see today?'"

Ian looked at Ann and
Ann looked at Ian.

They shrugged their shoulders
and said,

"Nothing."

About the Author

Photo courtesy of Jennifer Sickels.

Chris Sickels, the creative force behind award-winning Red Nose Studio, creates an eccentric world we'd all like to visit. Endearing characters and intricate sets draw you in with wit, intelligence and charm. His three-dimensional illustrations are built from a variety of materials. Sets and puppets are a combination of wire, fabric, cardboard, wood, miniatures, found objects and anything else within arms' reach.

Chris describes his magical work, saying "The sculptures sometimes look pretty crude, or the stitching is really rough, or the buildings are painted really sloppily. They're not poetic, there's no rhythm to them, there's no math to them. But that's how my work is. My work isn't really graceful. It's usually pretty awkward—like if the puppet moved, he'd fall, or he'd trip, or he'd run into a wall. It's a bit of beauty and a bit of awkwardness. And I think that's kind of how I am."

Red Nose Studio's illustrations appear in advertising, magazines, books, newspapers, packaging, character development and animation. His work has been honored by virtually every award institution or annual and has been featured in *HOW*, *Print*, *Creativity* and *3x3* Magazine, as well as in a number of art and design books including Taschen's *Illustration Now!* He has twice been honored with the Carol Anthony Grand Prize award from the Society of Illustrators 3-D Salon. Two of his short films, *The Red Thread Project* and *Innards*, were selected to screen at the 2005 and 2006 Los Angeles International Short Film Festival.